STEP-by-STEP
SCIENCE

Light and Dark

Chris Oxlade

Illustrated by Shirley Tourret
and Andrew Farmer

W
FRANKLIN WATTS
NEW YORK • LONDON • SYDNEY

First published in Great Britain by
Franklin Watts
96 Leonard Street
London
EC2A 4RH

Franklin Watts Australia
14 Mars Road
Lane Cove
NSW 2006
Australia

ISBN: 0 7496 2949 5
10 9 8 7 6 5 4 3 2 1
Dewey Decimal Classification 535
A CIP catalogue record for this book is available from the British Library
Printed in Dubai

Planning and production by Discovery Books Limited
Design: Ian Winton
Editor: Helena Attlee
Consultant: Jeremy Bloomfield

Photographs: Bryan and Cherry Alexander: page 13 bottom, 28 left;
(BON57666) A Family in a Candlelit Interior, 1852 (oil on panel) by Johannes Rosiere (1818-1901)
Bonhams, London/Bridgeman Art Library, London/New York: 13 top; Bruce Coleman: page 8 (Jane
Burton), 9 (Kim Taylor), 11 (M Fogden), 18 bottom (Hans-Peter Merten); Greg Evans: page 7 top right
and left, 12, 20; Eye Ubiquitous: page 6 (G Daniels); Chris Fairclough: page 18 top, 28 right; Robert
Harding Picture Library: page 7 bottom (James Strachan), 22 right (Victor Englebert); Image Bank:
page 16 (A T Willet), 19 (L Isy-Schwart), 24 (Carlos Navajos), 30 top (Larry Keenan Assoc); Planet
Earth Pictures: page 10; Science Picture Library: page 5 (Mehau Kulyk), 25 (Francoise Sauze),
30 bottom (Lawrence Livermore National Lab), 31 (Phillipe Plailly); Spectrum: cover;
Tony Stone Worldwide: page 14 (Barbara Filet), 17 (Doug Armand), 21 top (Charles Gupton),
22 left (David Hanson), 26 (Jeremy Horner), 27 (Darrell Gulin); Topham: page 21 bottom.

Contents

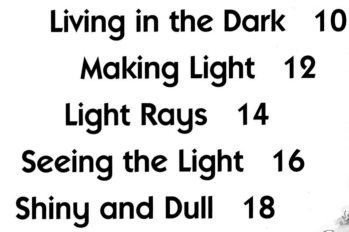

Light and Dark

What is the difference between day and night? The big difference is that it is usually light during the day and dark at night.

Daylight is made by the sun. Nearly all of the plants and animals on Earth need the sunlight to live and grow. Without the sun's heat and light the plants and animals in this picture would die.

Sunlight

The sun looks very, very bright, even though it is 150 million kilometres away from us. You must never look straight at the sun because it could damage your eyes.

Day and Night

The Earth is always spinning. The sun can only shine on the side of the Earth that is turned towards it. On this side of the Earth it is daytime. The other side of the Earth is in darkness and it is night.

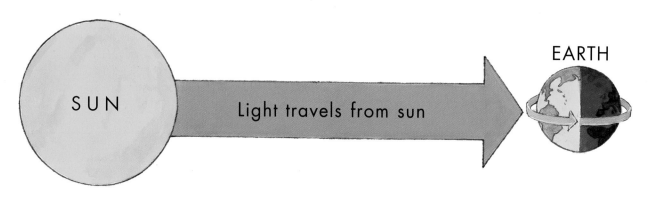

The different sides of the Earth have their day and night at different times.

Working the Night Shift

Most people work during the day. Some people have to work at night, when everyone else is asleep. These fire fighters have been called out to work in the middle of the night.

When people are eating breakfast in London...

...it is the middle of the night in New York. Most people are asleep.

At the same time, the sun is just setting over Fiji.

Night Life

Humans are not very good at seeing in the dark. Some animals are much better at seeing in dim light than we are. These animals come out at night and hunt for food. Even on moonless nights they can make use of the twinkling starlight.

Cats often hunt at night. The **pupils** of their eyes open very wide in the dark, letting in as much light as possible.

This owl sleeps during the day. At nightfall it comes out to hunt for food. Its huge eyes and sharp hearing help it to find rats, mice and young rabbits to eat.

Moths

Have you ever noticed that moths are attracted by lights at night? A moth usually relies on the moon to guide it as it flies. If it sees another light it becomes confused and it ends up flying in circles.

Living in the Dark

Many creatures spend most of their lives in complete darkness under the ground. Moles can hear quite well, but they are almost completely blind. This does not matter as there is no light under the ground and good eyesight would be useless.

Badgers sleep all day and hunt at night. They have poor eyesight but a good sense of smell.

Some creatures are able to make their own light. The deep-sea angler fish lives at the bottom of the ocean, where it is dark all the time. It has a long feeler attached to its head which has a glowing light on the end of it. This light attracts the small fish which are its food.

The earthworm has no eyes.

The mole uses its strong front legs and paws to dig tunnels deep under the ground.

Big Leaves

Plants need light to survive. In the deep shade of the rain forest there is very little light. Plants living on the forest floor have large leaves. This helps them to make good use of any light that does reach them.

Making Light

During the day, most of our light comes from the sun. When it is dark we have to make our own light. Most of the lights in our homes are powered by electricity. Electricity is used to light the streets as well. This picture shows a street in New York. It is lit up by thousands of coloured lights.

This picture (right) was painted by Johannes Rosiere 150 years ago, when candles or oil lamps were used to give light.

In some places, such as Norway (below), there are people who do not use electricity. This fire is being used to give light, as well as the heat needed for cooking.

Light Rays

Have you ever seen light shining through the trees of a forest in the early morning? In this picture you can see that light always travels in straight lines. These lines of light are called light rays.

TRAVELLING LIGHT

You can see light travelling in rays by using a torch and some talcum powder.

1 Spread a sheet of newspaper on the floor.

2 Hold a torch over the paper, pointing it at the wall.

3 Turn the torch on and then shake a little talcum powder into the air over the newspaper. Can you see the light rays in the powder?

14

Because light travels in straight lines, it cannot pass through the narrow, twisting entrance of this cave. The people inside the cave are called **pot-holers**. They must use torches to see where they are going.

Light travels faster than anything else in the universe. In a single second it can move 300,000 kilometres. It takes only 8 minutes for the light of the sun to travel 150 million kilometres to the Earth.

Seeing the Light

Have you ever wondered how we see things? We see things that make their own light, such as candles or light bulbs, because they send rays of light to our eyes. We call things that make their own light **luminous**.

Lightning creates a flash of bright light.

Most of the objects around us don't make light of their own. We see them because rays of light bounce off them and into our eyes. When light rays bounce we say that they are **reflected**.

You see everything in this picture of a market in Grenada (right) by reflected light. When it is completely dark we can't see at all. This is because there are no rays of light to be reflected by the objects around us.

Shiny and Dull

Some objects reflect light much better than others. How well an object reflects light depends on its surface. A smooth, light-coloured surface is a better reflector than a rough, dark-coloured one.

Light-coloured things, like these Greek houses (below), look bright because they reflect more of the light rays which hit them than dark-coloured things. A surface that reflects no light looks black.

Many things that are not smooth can also reflect light. The rough, rocky surface of the moon reflects the light of the sun.

Shining Through

Most materials reflect light rays, but some do not. When light rays hit glass or clear plastic, the light passes straight through. We call these **transparent** materials.

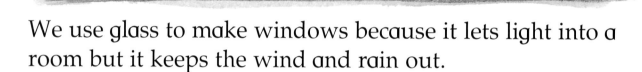

We use glass to make windows because it lets light into a room but it keeps the wind and rain out.

You can't see through paper, but it does let some light through. We say that materials like this are **translucent**. In Japan, the rooms of some houses are divided by paper screens.

Opaque materials stop light from passing through them. Most of the things we see around us are opaque.

During the Second World War, special opaque curtains were used to cover windows. This stopped light shining out into the street. Without lights to guide them, the enemy aircraft flying overhead did not know where to drop their bombs.

Making Shadows

On a sunny day you can see your shadow all of the time. You can run as fast as you like but you won't get rid of it!

What causes a shadow? The answer is simple. When you stand in the way of the sun's rays, you stop them reaching the ground on the other side of you. Because no light reaches the ground it is dark. This is a shadow.

Shadow Puppets

Many different countries in the world use shadow puppets to tell traditional stories. This puppet show is being performed in Indonesia.

MAKE A SHADOW PLAY

1 Decide on the story for your play. You could use a fairy tale or a new story of your own.

2 Cut the shapes of the characters from stiff card and use tape to stick each shape to a short stick or a pencil.

3 Hang a large white sheet over a bamboo cane. Ask your audience to sit down in front of the sheet.

4 Ask a friend to shine a torch onto the back of the sheet.

5 Hold your puppets up between the torch and the back of the sheet. When their shadows are in the right position, you are ready to start your play.

Long and Short Shadows

Early in the morning and late in the afternoon the sun is low in the sky. At these times of day the shadows cast by objects are very long.

In the middle of the day, when the sun is high in the sky, shadows are shorter.

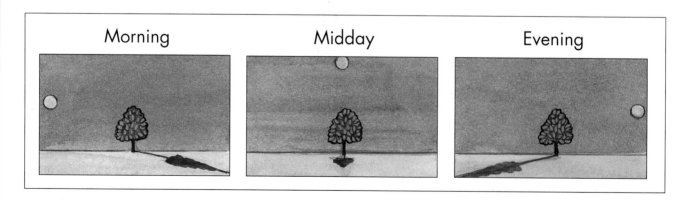

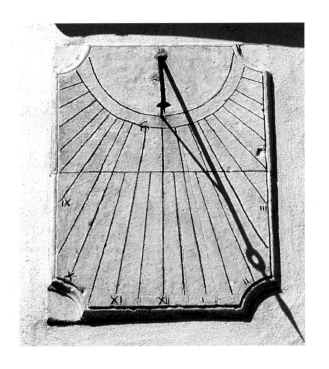

For many centuries people used sundials like this to tell the time. A sundial tells the time by using shadows. As the Earth spins and the sun appears to move across the sky, the upright part of the sundial makes a shadow which moves around the dial.

MAKE A SHADOW CLOCK

Find an open place, where there are no trees or tall buildings between you and the sun.

1 Push a straight stick into the ground.

2 Make a neat hole in the middle of a sheet of white card. Put it over the stick so that it rests on the ground.

3 Mark the position of the stick's shadow on the paper. The shadow will change position as the sun moves across the sky. Mark its position every hour as the day goes by and write the time by it.

4 Try using your shadow clock the following day to tell the time.

Mirrors

Mirrors reflect light better than anything else. You can see a perfect picture of yourself in a flat mirror. This picture is called a reflection.

In the hall of mirrors at the fairground, the mirrors have curved surfaces. This is why they give such strange reflections.

A mirror reflects nearly all the light rays that hit it. Most mirrors are made from a sheet of glass. The back of the glass is painted with silver paint, making a smooth, shiny surface. Before glass mirrors were invented, people used mirrors made from polished metal.

FUN WITH MIRRORS

1 Look at your reflection in a mirror. Move your right hand. Which hand moves in your reflection? Mirrors always swap left and right like this.

2 Write your name in capital letters on a sheet of paper. Hold it up to the mirror. What happens?

3 Now try to write your name so that it will look correct in the mirror. This is called mirror writing.

Mirror Image

The still water of this lake gives an almost perfect reflection.

Bending Light

When light moves from one material to another it slows down. This makes the rays of light bend. We call this **refraction**.

Refracted light can play tricks on us. It makes this paintbrush look broken.

Refraction can make things look closer to us under the water than they really are. This fisherman has to be very clever to catch a fish with his spear.

Lenses

Light bends when it goes from air into glass. The lenses in a telescope bend all of the light rays together. This makes things look closer than they really are.

Laser Light

The bright lights going up into the sky in this picture are called laser beams. Lasers make very narrow beams of extremely bright light which travel a long way without spreading out.

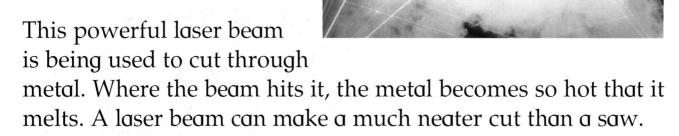

This powerful laser beam is being used to cut through metal. Where the beam hits it, the metal becomes so hot that it melts. A laser beam can make a much neater cut than a saw.

Laser beams travel in perfectly straight lines. When the Channel Tunnel between France and England was built, surveyors used a laser beam to check that the tunnel was being drilled accurately.

Holograms

Lasers can be used to make beautiful **holograms** like this one. Most credit cards have holograms on them. This makes them very difficult to forge.

Glossary

Hologram: A picture which has been made by using lasers. Although it is flat, it seems to be three dimensional

Lightning: A huge spark which jumps between the ground and the clouds during a thunderstorm

Luminous: Something which makes its own light is luminous

Opaque: An opaque material does not allow any light to pass through it

Pot-holer: A person who explores caves and underground passages

Pupils: The small holes at the front of the eyes. The pupil lets light into the eye

Reflected: When light bounces off something we say that it has been reflected. The picture that you see in a mirror is called a reflection

Refraction: Light rays bend as they go from one material into another. This is called refraction

Translucent: A translucent material allows some light to pass through it. You can't see clearly through something that is translucent

Transparent: A transparent material allows most of the light to pass through it. You can see clearly through transparent materials

Index